Performance Appraisal
Tools and Techniques

SirajuddinChougle

DEDICATION

This book is dedicated to my best friend

Dr. Abdul Majid Ansari

and

our life-long friendship

which has stood the test of time.

ACKNOWLEDGEMENTS

My grateful thanks are due to:

1. Allah for giving me this opportunity to write this book.

2. My family who gave me the full liberty to continue my work without disturbing and demanding my time.

3. Dr. Abdul Majid Ansari for overlooking my work time and again.

4. The publishers for undertaking the publication and sale of the book.

Sirajuddin Chougle

PREFACE

Performance Appraisal is a yearly practice in organizations around the world. The purpose is to evaluate the employees overall performance during that assessment year. The HR Department of many organizations uses it as a tool to take decisions relating to increment, placement and promotion etc. of the employee.

This book on Performance Appraisal is a concise handy reference for both the appraiser and the appraisee. Thisannual practice which is a must routine in most of the organizations is many times dreaded by the appraisee, as if it is an annual examination in which one should come out in flying colors.

In many parts formats are taken from VNG International Co-operation Agency of the Association of Netherlands Municipalities, Virginia Commonwealth University and University of Northern Iowa for better presentation. The book is a ready reckoner for the students and also a quick go-through during the examination when students are under stress. My best wishes to all readers seeking benefit from this book.

Author

CONTENTS

1.Goals and Standards

Let us understand the meaning of goals and standards, terminologies often used in management. They have a definite meaning which every worker should be able to imbibe in their vocabulary.

A. Goal

A Goal is a statement of results which are to be achieved or in other words it is the purpose toward which an endeavor is directed with a definite outcome.

Goals describe three important attributes:

i.*Conditions:* that will exist when the desired outcome has been accomplished;

ii.*Time frame*: during which the outcome is to be completed; and

iii.*Resources:* that the organization is willing to commit to achieve the desired result.

In simple words goals have to be challenging, but at the same time they should be achievable and established with the participation of those responsible for meeting them.

Let us explain it with an example:

'Increase the flow of takeaway parcels through the Parcel counter to a minimum of 200 per day from 1st January. The total cost to accomplish this should not exceed Rs.2,000/-.'

Once accomplished, a new goal can be established to emphasis the next set of desired results.

B. Standards

A standard is referred to an ongoing performance criterion that must be met time and time again. Standards are usually expressed quantitatively, and refer to such things as attendance, breakage, manufacturing tolerances, production rates and safety standards. They are most effective when established with the participation of those who must meet them.

An example will make it clear:

'The departmental filing back log should not exceed three days. Any record requested should be available within five minutes of the request'.

In general, goals apply more to managers and professional employees who engage in individualized projects. Standards are more common for workers engaged in routine, repetitive tasks.

When employees participate in setting goals and standards, there should be no mystery about how their performance will be judged. Employees cannot say, 'why didn't you tell me that's what you wanted?' or, 'who dreamed up these impossible standards?' Since goals and/or standards are the primary criteria by which performance will be measured, it is worth reviewing them.

Identifying Goals and Standards

In the following list of statements, identify which is goal and standard?

If the statement is neither a goal nor a standard, leave the statement.

i. Breakage in the laboratory should be kept to a minimum.

ii. Eliminate maintenance coding errors for existing computer programs by 31 December, at a cost not to exceed 30 working hours.

iii. Reduce the cost of ongoing operations by 1 January.

iv. Telephones are to be answered immediately and messages taken when necessary.

v. To reduce burner maintenance cost by 10 percent before 30 November, at a once and for all cost not to exceed ` 15,000/-

vi. To increase sales of men's watches by 15 percent during Diwali season, with no increase in costs.

vii. Appreciably reduce time lost because of accidents by year end.

viii. Errors in recording class enrolment will not exceed 2% of the total monthly enrolment.

ix. Telephones should be answered after no more than two rings. Telephone manners are expected to follow those prescribed

3

in the company handbook. Messages should include date, time of call, relevant names and numbers, and the nature of the call.

x. To increase Western Region sales by ` 300,000/-, by year end, at an increased cost of sales of less than 4 percent.

2.Performance Appraisals

Introduction

Evaluation of staff as an ongoing process is a need of every organization whether from organized or unorganized sector, small or big, and even legal or illegal. Performance appraisal is a technique which when used positively helps individual staff to identify their strengths and weakness, overcome challenges and be prepared for opportunities. The process can help develop their overall temperament and performance and boost their morale. It leads towards improvement in the organizational performance and growth. It benefits both the staff and the organization. Usually it is an annual task undertaken by the organization.

This annual exercise of performance appraisals enables the managements to take various decisions on the basis of its outcome. First of all its helps the management to generate confidence in the staff as it agree upon their expectation and accordingly sets objectives. It sets monitoring standards; delegation of responsibilities and tasks thus feeds the business planning process. Further it identifies and establishes appropriate training need for individual and organizational training needs, annual pay and grading reviews and analysis and planning for the coming year.

It is through performance appraisal that the management is able to develop career and succession planning for individual staff, review performance against set objectives and standards agreed upon in the previous year appraisal meeting. It helps in motivating the staff, attitude and behavioral development, communicating and at the same time aligning individual and organizational aims and most important fostering positive relationship between the management and the staff.

Performance appraisal in whatever form it is taken it is vital for managing the performance of the people and the organization. It leads to planning for the future development of both i.e. the people and the organization. The annual appraisal is the only time that both the parties the management on one side and the employees on the other side sit together even if they dislike the formalities. The process is seen as stressful exercise, daunting and emotionally challenging on both sides. But appraisals are easier if both sides trust each other.

To ease the process the authorities need to develop a cordial atmosphere round the year. Why sit only at the end of the year to undertake appraisals? Why not sit as often as possible? Communication with each other will tend to break barriers, develop relationships and thereby when actual appraisals take place it will be much more natural, easy and quick and yes more productive.

Appraisals should avoid discrimination against anyone on the ground of age, gender, race, religion, disability etc. It should not become a tool in the hands of the appraiser to take revenge or extract favors. The UK Employment Equality (Age) Regulations 2006, (consistent with Europe), effective from 1st October 2006, make it particularly important to avoid any comments, judgments, suggestions, questions or decisions which might be perceived by the appraise to be biased.

The appraisals should address the 'whole person' development and not just job skills or for that matter skills required for the next promotion. The employer should recognize that helping the employee to grow as a 'whole person' will promote positive attitudes, motivate the employee, develop new skills that could surprisingly increase the efficiency and productivity of the employee benefitting the organization. This leads to reducing workers turnover, retain the best staff and also become attractive destination for new recruits.

Ways to make Performance appraisal manageable and effective:
Appraisal is generally done at the end of the year. The face to face assessment becomes a marathon meeting. Ideally it is suggested that it can be done over the year. The superior can communicate with the subordinate one-to-one on monthly or quarterly basis about the activities, ideas performance progress etc. over a cup of coffee. This will make the annual appraisal a manageable affair in limited time.

Performance appraisals should be made a positive and fruitful experience for both the appraiser and the appraisee. All efforts should be made to build it into 'looked forward' event. The process should provide a platform for fostering development and motivation for positive progress. A hind of precaution, that the performance appraisal should not be used like a weapon against the person which could develop fear or resentment. It should never be used to handle matters of discipline or admonishment that should be handled through separate meetings.
To encourage the use of appraisal performance report for the benefit of both the organization and the employee it is necessary to make both the appraiser and the appraisee aware of its important in advance. If necessary short training can also be fruitful, this trains how to use appraisal process properly.

3.Attitudes and Performance Appraisals

A Well Planned Performance Appraisal

Performance appraisal is not taken seriously but just as a routine job by people who are responsible for performance appraisals. They often assign a low priority to it because they are not aware about the benefits of a good appraisal session. Some advantages of doing a professional appraisal on a regular basis are given below.

Valuable insights gained through performance appraisal:

i.One to one good communication during appraisal reveals about job expectations, this leads to discovery of new ideas and improved methods.

ii.Good job appraising performance reduces the anxiety of the employees as they know how they are doing.

iii.When employees receive regular corrective feedback on their performanceit increases productivity.

iv.It leads to reinforcing sound work practices and encourage good performance when theirpositive contributions is publicly recognize.

v.Encouraging two way communications with employees clarifies goals and they now seem beto be achievable and likely to be exceeded.

vi.Regular appraisal sessions remove surprises about how the quality of work is being perceived.

vii. Learning to conduct professional performance appraisals is excellent preparation for advancement and increased responsibility.

The appraiser should sit across with open mind without any prejudice about the appraisee to get best results. Chances are that the appraiser will face these three options:

Option 1 I know the Best

Option 2 I will set the Goals, you meet them

Option 3 Let us review the work together, establish some realistic Goals and Evaluate performance accordingly

Which one you will prefer? But natural it should be the third option for better results.

Thought Stimulators for Self-appraisal[1]

When going for performance appraisal the appraisee should prepare oneself for the event. This can be done by undertaking self-appraisal. The questions given under can help you prepare for your

---

[1]Resemblance of format to: Employee relations and performance management, Virginia Commonwealth University; www.hr.vcu.edu

performance appraisal. As you read each question, think about your performance, your progress, and your plans for future growth.

i. What critical abilities does my job require? To what extent do I fulfill them?

ii. What do I like best about my job? Least?

iii. What were my specific accomplishments during this appraisal period?

iv. Which goals or standards did I fall short of meeting?

v. How could my supervisor help me do a better job?

vi. Is "there anything that the organization or my supervisor does that hinders my effectiveness?

vii. What changes would improve my performance?

viii. Does my present job make the best use of my capabilities? How could I become more productive?

ix. Do I need more experience or training in any aspect of my current job? How could it be accomplished?

x. What have I done since my last appraisal to prepare myself for more responsibility?

xi. What new goals and standards should be established for the next appraisal period? Which old ones need to be modified or deleted?

xii. What do I expect to be doing five years from now?

Avoid pitfalls in Appraisal Process:

i. **Bias/Prejudice**: Things we tend to react to that have nothing to do withperformance such as: race, religion, education, family background, age and/ or sex.

ii. **Trait assessment**: Too much attention to characteristics that have nothing to do with the job and are difficult to measure. Examples include characteristics such as flexibility, sincerity, or friendliness.

iii. **Over-emphasis:** Emphasizing on favorable or unfavorable performance of one or two tasks which could lead to an unbalanced evaluation of the overall contribution.

iv. **Impression:** Relying on impressions rather than facts.

v. **Unwarranted Responsibility**: Holding the employee responsible for the effect of factors beyond his or her control.

vi. **No time to prepare:** Failure to provide each employee with an opportunity for advance preparation.

vii. **Performance Measurement:** Concentrate on performance measured against mutually understood expectations.

Developing an Action Plan for Appraisal Guidelines:

i. Don't cover too many areas in one discussion. Concentrate on those which deserve the most attention.

ii. Make sure there are specific, unbiased examples that can be used to support your points but that also allow for dialogue.

iii.Develop positive approaches to correcting problems. Give the employee an opportunity to suggest solutions before any final decisions are made.

iv.Be prepared to provide praise and positive reinforcement for items which deserve it.

v.Identify developmental activities that will improve the employee's performance in the present assignment; and/or provide preparation for future assignments.

vi.Note any projects, goals and/or standards to be accomplished during the forthcoming appraisal period. Discuss them and reach agreement on them during the session.

vii.Plan to involve the employee in all aspects of the discussion.

4.How to Begin the Appraisal Discussion

Managers have the responsibility to initiate appraisal discussions. Although individual personalities will influence the format, experts agree that the discussion should be held in a private place to avoid interruptions and should begin on a positive and friendly note. While chit-chat will help break the ice, both parties will welcome getting down to business.

One way to accomplish this is to highlight a specific positive achievement and discuss it first. Another approach is to ask the employee to review his or her accomplishments for the appraisal period. This allows the employee to select where to begin and can lead to a candid assessment of actual performance. While the employee is talking, the leader should be an interested listener.

If variances between expectations and results are evident, it is important that both leader and employee try to find out what they are and why they occurred. This helps the discussion become a joint problem solving session which can lead to the implementation of effective solutions.

The employee should be encouraged to identify as many reasons for variances as possible. None should be rejected out of hand even if they seem to be excuses. The leader should also contribute possible causes so that nothing significant is over- looked. This sharing allows for an exchange of viewpoints. This can provide better insights for all concerned and lead to a new understanding of the expectations of theorganization, and the people who staff it.

Discussing Unsatisfactory Performance

Employees who work in a non-threatening atmosphere are more likely to discuss their shortcomings in the appraisal selling. When this occurs, the supervisor can be supportive by saying something like, 'That's very perceptive. What can we do to correct this situation?'

If the employee has been unsatisfactory in an aspect of his or her job, and does not bring up areas of weak performance, the supervisor must do so. It helps to be able to describe the impact of the poor performance on the organization.

Some employees may not realize they are falling short of expectations. Or they may assume everything is acceptable because no one has ever discussed the problem with them. Sometimes they may feel everything is OK because they see others doing the same thing.

A first step to correct unsatisfactory performance is to review expectations. If the employee is unaware of these expectations, they must be made clear, and a commitment made that they will be met. If expectations are not being met for some other reason, the supervisor must first learn why, and then agree on a corrective action plan worked out with the employee.

Questions like these can be helpful in opening up the issues:
   i.'Are you aware of the standards for quantity and quality we expect on this item?'
   ii.'Are you aware of your error rate versus the departmental average?'
   iii.'We seem to be running about two weeks behind schedule; can you tell me why, and what we can do to catch up?'
   iv.'Your sales reports are excellent but they are never on time. Can you explain why?'
   v.'Fifty per cent of your staff resigned in the last quarter. To what do you attribute that?'

How to Get an Employee to Talk Freely[2]

Employees often say very little during an appraisal discussion. There are several possible reasons for this, some include:

    a. The employee does not understand the purpose of the appraisal, and is afraid to express an opinion.

    b. The employee is not given the opportunity to express an opinion.

    c. The employee was not given time to prepare for the discussion.

    d. The employee's thoughts and ideas are quickly brushed aside or discounted.

    e. The employee feels the whole process is meaningless.

A manager can overcome this reluctance to enter into a dialogue by creating the right type of non-threatening atmosphere. The methods are given below:

1. Be descriptive rather than judgmental

When a supervisor is judgmental about an employee's performance, it al- most always brings out defensive behavior. A better climate is

---

[2]Resemblance of format to: Internal Management, a Process of Change, VNG International Co-operation Agency of the Association of Netherlands Municipalities; www.vng-international.nl

established when descriptive terms are used to describe problems. This makes it possible for the leader and employee to discuss a solution unemotionally, or even better, a solution generated by the employee. Note the differences in the following example:

Judgmental	Descriptive
'How could you do such a silly thing?'	'Can you explain what caused the incident?'

Leaders who use descriptive, non-judgmental language in the appraisal discussion show a desire to analyse and resolve a problem, not to find a scapegoat or a way to demean the employee.

2. Be supportive, not authoritarian

Supervisors sometimes purposely, and sometimes inadvertently, display an authoritarian attitude during the discussion. This can create resentment and defensiveness. It is usually better to respect theemployee's ability to contribute to the solution of a problem. Here is an example:

Authoritarian	Supportive
Here is what we will doto get this done on time'.	'What do you suggest we do to get this done ontime

in the future?

Supportive practices generate options for problem-solving because the employee is encouraged to make suggestions. They also focus on the problem, not the employee. In addition, a supportive approach promotes better listening by both parties, and permits a climate where disagreement is not only acceptable but invited.

3. Reflect equality, not superiority

Supervisors who put too much emphasis on their position and power often create barriers between themselves and their employees. Supervisors who share information with employees and then seek their opinions provide a flavor of equality. Here is an example:

Superiority	Equality
'I was doing it this way before you were born.'	'We have done it this way for years but I would like to hear your ideas on how we can do it better.'

Employees appreciate a leader who shares information, asks for opinions andlistens to ideas. Leaders who understand this have appraisal discussions that aremore enlightening and productive.

4. Be accepting, not dogmatic:

Supervisors who approach decisions, plans and problems dogmatically are telling employees there is no need for other ideas or solutions. Things have already been decided. This can demoralize an employee who has ideas and wants to excel. Leaders who listen to employee input, or allow their ideas to be challenged in a search for the best solution, stimulate enthusiasm, creativity and productivity. Here is an example that contrasts the two approaches:

Dogmatic	**Accepting**
'This is the best solution.'	'This is the best solution I could come up with. What other possibilities do you see?'

The Procedure in a Nutshell

1. **Preparation for Appraisal**: First and foremost keep all necessary records of the appraisee ready, which includes previous performance appraisal documents, performance records, achievements and all such documents. If there is a self-appraisal form get it filled well in advance.

2.Information: Inform the appraisee about the date, time and venue of the appraisal well in advance. This will give the appraisee sufficient time to prepare for the event.

3.Proper venue and layout: Suitable venue should be selected for the appraisal which is easily accessible and free from interruption. The layout should be relaxing and pleasing. Set comfortable sitting arrangement which makes the whole process an un-stressful and relax-full experience. It is advisable that to have a meeting table and easy chair, but avoid face to face set-up as it is a confrontational position

Actual Performance appraisal:

    i.Opening: The appraiser should make the appraisee comfortable by warm and friendly welcome and with positive opening statements, like, 'how are you?' Encourage discussion rather than one sided monologue. Keep on reminding the appraisee about the benefits of the process for his future progress. Simultaneously record important points which will help you to make appropriate evaluation later on when the process is over.

ii. Reviews and action plan: Evaluate the performance of the appraisee on the basis of available evidence. Resist judging the appraisee, rather let the fact and figures talk. Find out the aspiration of the appraisee and how best it will be possible to achieve them. At the same time also tell the expectations from the organization. Accordingly draw-up action plan with mutual agreement which are realistic and that meets the goals and objectives of the organization.

iii. Support system: The appraisee may require support system to achieve the set objectives. This is basically the training and monitoring. Discuss likely training requirement keeping in mind the 'whole person development' concept. Do not commit something which the organization will not be able to fulfill.

iv. Close positively: Before thanking the appraisee make sure that he has nothing more to say from his side. Show concern about it and invite him to share something which he may still be holding back. Once done, thank him for his contribution to the progress of the organization. Commit to helping him when required.

v.Follow-up: Ensure that all necessary notes are finalized and documents are filed and also relevant documents are send to various departments if required.

5.Questions That Facilitate Appraisal Discussions

There are three types of question that can be used to help the Appraiser andAppraised better understand each other's point of view.

1. Open questions: Questions which cannot be answered with a yes or no.

These questions require an opinion or expression of feeling.

For example:

'What is your opinion of Mr. A?'

Advantages of open questions include:

    i.demonstration of your interest in the other person's point of view;

    ii.confirmation that you value the other person's ideas and feelings;

    iii.stimulation of thought about specific issues;

    iv.better understanding of the other person's needs;

    v.encouragement of a dialogue rather than a monologue.

2. Reflective questions: A reflective question repeats a statement that the other person has made in the form of a question. Good listening skills" are required. It is also important to select the most significant feeling or idea stated.

For example:

Employee: 'Our results would be better if we modified the procedures used to take samples.'

Supervisor: 'You're convinced the results can be improved?'

Arguments can be avoided. You respond without accepting or rejecting what has been said, for:

  a. It confirms you understand what has been said. If you reflect incorrectly, the other party has an opportunity to correct you.

  b. The other person is encouraged to clarify or expand upon what has he in mind.

  c. The other person can recognise illogical statements they may have made if the statement comes back in a non-directive fashion.

  d. They create a dialogue conducive to agreement.

3. Directive questions: These are used to solicit information about a particular point or issue. Directive questions are usually reserved until after the other person has finished talking on the subject. Directive questions can then be used to sustain communication, or obtain information or ideas in which you are specifically interested.

Here is an example:

Supervisor: 'If you are convinced the results can be improved, what steps would you take and when would you take them?'

Directive questions have these advantages:

　i.They provide pertinent information in those areas of greatest importance to you.

　ii.They challenge the other person to explore ideas, defend statements, and contribute suggestions.

　iii.They offer both parties specific facts on an issue.

Open, reflective and directive questions are all useful techniques to draw theemployee into a thorough discussion of job performance and personal development.

The appraisal discussion is more than a simple review of job performance. It should progress naturally to a discussion of how the employee can do a better job in the future.It is also a good time to draw out the employee's ambitions and aspirations.

6.Personal Developments and Growth

As performance is discussed, it often becomes apparent that additional training and development are required or desirable. It is also possible that the discussion will provide an indication that an employee is ready for more responsibility which re- quires new or improved skills.

Therefore, specific areas for improvement, and the need for new skill development should be discussed. Techniques by which further growth can be accomplished should also be covered. The leader should encourage the employee to talk about personal growth needs, so goals to meet them can be established. This effort can be supported by:

  i.Serving as a sounding board to explore developmental alternatives.
  ii.Testing the extent to which the employee has thought through developmental objectives.
  iii.Providing a supportive climate for learning.

The final employee development plans should be specific and include agreement by the employee for:

i. What the employee needs to do.

ii. When the employee needs to do it.

iii. What the leader needs to do and when.

iv. Once development is completed, how it is to be applied.

Closing the Appraisal Discussion

When the appraiser and appraiser and employee have concluded discussion of past performance, addressed any development needs and established new goals and/or standards for the future, they need to take time to review these agreements and plans. Many performance reviews fail because both the appraiser and appraise end the session with differing perceptions about what was accomplished and whatwas agreed. To prevent this appraiser should conclude the discussion by:

i. Summarizing what has been discussed and agreed. This should be done positively and enthusiastically.

ii. Giving the employee a chance to react, question, and add additional ideas and suggestions.

iii. Expressing appreciation for the employee's participation and reinforcing the commitment to future plans.

iv. Following the discussion with a written record of the agreements and/or required action plans.

Post Appraisal - Follow up

1. Written records

Once the performance appraisal discussion has been concluded, a managershould immediately make a written record of:

   i.the overall appraisal for the previous period;

  ii.plans which both parties agreed to;

 iii.any personal commitments requiring specific action.

    A copy of this summary should be given to the employee.

2. Reflection

Following each review is a good time to review your performance in leading the discussion. Some good questions are:

   a.What was done well?

   b.What was done poorly?

   c.What will be done differently next time?

   d.What was learned about the employee?

   e.What was learned about self and job?

3. Follow through

A third element of follow-up is to ensure that agreements are kept and plansfollowed.' If this is not done, the entire appraisal loses its impact and theemployee assumes no one cares very much about performance. This phase of the follow-up is actually the initial phase of the next appraisal.

A Performance Appraisal Checklist for Managers[3]

The following checklist is designed to guide the manager in preparing, conducting and following through employee performance appraisal discussions.

1. Personal preparation

    i.I have reviewed mutually understood expectations with respect to job duties, projects, goals, standard, and any other predetermined performance factors pertinent to this appraisal discussion.

    ii.I have observed job performance measured against mutually understood expectations. In so doing, I have done my best to avoid such pitfalls as :

        a.Bias/prejudice

        b.The vagaries of memory

        c.Over-attention to some aspects of the job at the expense of others

---

[3]Resemblance of format to: Supervisor Performance Appraisal Checklists, University of Northern Iowa; www.uni.edu

d. being influenced too much by my own experience

e. Trait evaluation rather than performance measurement

iii. I have reviewed the employee's background including:

a. Skills

b. Work experience

c. Training

iv. I have identified the employee's performance strengths and areas in need of improvement and in so doing have:

a. Accumulated specific, unbiased documentation that can be used to help communicate my position

b. Limited myself to those critical points that are the most important

c. Prepared a possible development plan in case the employee needs assistance in coming up with a suitable plan

v. I have identified areas for concentration in setting goals and standards for the next appraisal period.

vi. I have given the employee advance notice of when the discussion will be held so that he or she can prepare.

vii. I have set aside an adequate block of uninterrupted time to permit a full and complete discussion.

2. Conducting the appraisal discussion

i. I plan to begin the discussion by creating a sincere, but open and friendly atmosphere. This includes:

a. Reviewing the purpose of the discussion

b. Making it clear that it is a joint discussion for the purpose of mutualproblem-solving and goal setting

c. Striving to put the employee at ease

ii. In the body of the discussion I intend to keep the focus on job performance and related factors. This includes:

a. Discussing job requirements - employee strengths, accomplishments,improvement needs and evaluating results of performance against objectives set during previous reviews and discussions.

b. Being prepared to cite observations for each point I want to discuss

c. Encouraging the employee to appraise his or her own performance

d. Using open, reflective and directive questions to

promote thought, understanding and problem solving

iii.I will encourage the employee to outline his or her personal plans for self- development before suggesting ideas of my own. In the process, I will :

    a.Try to get the employee to set personal growth and improvement targets.

    b.Strive to reach agreement on appropriate development plans whichdetail what the employee intends to do, a timetable, and support I am prepared to give.

iv.I am prepared to discuss work assignment, projects and goals for the next appraisal period and will ask the employee to come prepared with suggestions.

3. Closing the discussion

I will be prepared to make notes during the discussion for the purpose of summarizing agreements and follow up. In closing, I will:

    a.Summaries what has been discussed

    b.Show enthusiasm for plans that have been made

c. Give the employee an opportunity to make additional suggestions

d. End on a positive, friendly, harmonious note

4. Post-appraisal follow-up

i. As soon as the discussion is over, I will record the plans made, points requiring follow-up, the commitments I made, and provide a copy for the employee,

ii. I will also evaluate how I handled the discussion.

a. What I did well.

b. What I could have done better.

c. What I learned about the employee and his or her job.

d. What I learned about myself and my job.

7.Forbidden Fruits

Characteristics of an Effective Appraiser

The following personal characteristics support effective performance appraisals.

This scale will help identify your strengths, and indicate areas where improvement would be beneficial. Circle the number that best reflects where you fall on the scale. The higher the number, the more the characteristic describes you. When you have finished, total the numbers circled in the space provided.

Sr. No.	Characteristics	Scale									
1	I like being responsible for productivity	10	9	8	7	6	5	4	3	2	1
2	I like people, and enjoy talking to them	10	9	8	7	6	5	4	3	2	1
3	I don't mind giving	10	9	8	7	6	5	4	3	2	1

	criticism of a constructive nature.										
4	I give praise freely when it is earned.	10	9	8	7	6	5	4	3	2	1
5	I am not intimidated by any subordinates who tell me what they really think	10	9	8	7	6	5	4	3	2	1
6	I seek new ideas and use them whenever possible.	10	9	8	7	6	5	4	3	2	1
7	I respect the knowledge and skill of the people who work for me.	10	9	8	7	6	5	4	3	2	1
8	I follow up to be sure commitments, goals and standards are being met.	10	9	8	7	6	5	4	3	2	1
9	I am sensitive to the needs and feelings of	10	9	8	7	6	5	4	3	2	1

	others.										
10	I am not worried by employees who know more about their work than I do.	10	9	8	7	6	5	4	3	2	1

Total =

Situation 1

The employee agrees with the appraisal and wants to improve. Some genuine differences of opinion are expressed, but the employee makes positive efforts to clarify the issues rather than be defensive.

Your

response:_____

_____

_____

_____

Situation 2

The employee does not accept responsibility for his standard performance and blames company politics and other employees.

Your

response_____

_____

_____

_____

Situation 3

The employee disagrees with elements of your appraisal and offers specific information to refute your findings.

Your   response

_____

_____

_____

_____

Situation 4

The employee accepts the appraisal without saying a word and prepares to leave before you have discussed the next performance plan.

Your

response_____

_____

_____

8.Performance Counselling

Definition:

Performance counseling can be defined as the help provided by an appraiser to his appraises in analyzing their performance and other job behavior in order to increase their job effectiveness.

It focuses on the analysis of performance on the job and identification oftraining needs for further development.

Objectives:

i. Helping him to realize his potential as a manager.

ii. Helping him to understand himself - his strengths and his weaknesses.

iii. Providing him an opportunity to acquire more insight into his behavior and analyze the dynamics of such behavior.

iv. Helping him to have better understanding of the environment.

v. Increasing his personal and interpersonal effectiveness by giving him feedback about his behavior and assisting him in analyzing his inter-personal competence.

vi. Encouraging him to set goals for further improvement.

vii. Encouraging him to generate alternatives for dealing with various problems.

Conditions for Effective Counselling

i. General climate of openness and mutuality.

ii. General helpful and empathic attitude of management.

iii. Sense of uninhibited participation by the subordinates in the performance review process.

iv. Dialogic relationship in goal setting and performance review.

v. Focus on work-oriented behavior.

vi. Focus on work-related problems and difficulties.

vii. A voidance of discussion of salary and other rewards.

Benefits of Counselling

i. It helps both of them to understand their strengths and weaknesses.

ii. Provides an opportunity to acquire more insight into their behavior and analyses dynamics of such behavior.

iii. Helps them to provide better understanding their environment.

iv. It helps them to increase their personal and inter-personal effectiveness through giving and receiving feedback about their behavior.

v.Guilds in mutual trust and confidence.

vi.Provides opportunity to share and discuss tensions, conflicts, concerns and problems in an empathic environment.

vii.Provides an opportunity to generate alternate solutions and implement them with a mutual understanding and support.

viii.Encourages setting goals for further improvement.

ix.Helps realize the-innate potential.

x.If the dyadic relationships are strong across the organization, theorganizational effectiveness will attain excellence.

Three Phases of Counselling

The three skills thatare important in Performance Counselling are:

1.Keying

2.Responding

3. Guiding

1. Keying

Keying refers to "reading" or tuning in accurately to people. The

Manager tries to understand the subordinate's frame of reference so as to perceive what the employee means by his verbal message.

Keying is achieved by undistorted perception of the other person and a reduction of noises and distraction and use of appropriate frame of reference. Therefore,keying requires the Manager to pay attention to the person to whom he is talking and recognizing his goals tram his point of view. This involves attending and listening.

When the Manager is conversing with an employee he must decide whether he wants to show that he is interested of disinterested in what the employee says. If he decides to show interest he must communicate the same by removal of physical barriers and distractions. This would mean not attending to phone calls,mails, visitors and colleagues, and giving all attention to the interview. Itwould also involve holding the discussion away from the noise to reduce anxiety.

Physical attending, therefore would mean putting aside whatever would distract the superior or the helper from giving his attention to the subordinate. It also calls for a genuine posture of involvement. If one notices two persons communicating in a serious conversation, one would notice the closeness with which each oneof them leans towards the other.

Specifically physical attending means:
a. Facing the other person squarely and conveying through that "I am available to you".
b. Eye contact communicates interest. The Counsellor or Superiorshould look directly at the client or subordinate.

The goal of the counsellor in the keying phase is to attend to the other, bothphysically and psychologically and to give himself entirely to being with the other.

"Attending" carefully to another involves lot of energy and demands a great deal of effort on the part of the counsellor. Although "attending" is a requisite for the pre-helping and keying stage, it should be prevalent in the other phases of Counselling. i.e. Responding and Guiding.

2. Responding

"Responding" is another skill wherein the manager communicates back to theemployee what he has learnt from "keying" which adds to, subtracts from or interchanges with the "meaning" the employee has communicated. The goal of the counsellor in this phase is to respond to the subordinate what he has to say, with respect and empathy, with a view to establish a relationship between the two that would facilitate the subordinate's self-exploration of the problem.

"Responding" primarily helps the manager to check his perception against theemployee. There are four aspects that are involved in "responding". They are:

i. Empathy:

A person is accurately empathic when he can do two things:

(a) get inside the other person, look at the world through the frame of reference of this other person, get a feeling about the world what the other is like, and

(b) communicate this understanding to the other in such a manner that the subordinate knows that the superior has understood both his feelings and the behavior and experience underlying these feelings.

The long range goal in Empathy is to communicate with the subordinate thedepth of understanding in him and his predicament to enable him to expand and clarify his own self-understanding as well as understanding of the others.

While the counsellor hits the mark in terms of empathy the subordinate is ableto move forward and begin exploring further dimensions of the problem.

ii. Respect:

Respect is a particular way of viewing the other person. In fact, "respect" means valuing another person simply because he is a human being. It conveys that being a human being has a value in itself. In a counselling situation this iscommunicated to us where the superior orients himself towards and decides to work with the subordinate. "Orientation towards" is comprised of attitudes which must be translated into concrete behavior and is a display of attitude wherein the subordinate feels that the superior "cares" for him.

iii. Genuineness:

Genuineness refers to congruence and lack of disparity between what one feels about another person and about what one communicates to him

iv. Concreteness:

Concreteness is being specific and factual. Since the entire counselling isdirected towards self-exploration and action, it is essential that self-exploration be concrete. Unless problems are discussed in operational and concrete terms, it is difficult to solve them. Vague problems would lead to vague solutions. Concreteness requires both the superior and the subordinate to avoid the process of "rambling". This would be necessary to achieve a certain degree of direction in the counselling process which would be difficult in a long story telling.Another way in which the counsellor can be concrete is to ask directly specificinformation, particularly on information which is vague. If the subordinate really does not know the reason why his performance is low, it is possible that he will make up answers to satisfy the superior. The cause of things, especially remote causes are seldom evident. The subordinate can talk endlessly about causes but this does not lead to the kind of insight, which leads to action program.

"Responding" may be done at two levels -- a feeling level and a meaning level.Recognizing the feelings of the other person, playing it back or checking with him or paraphrasing them etc., are ways of responding to feeling. For example when a person says, "This job is really terrible, I had looked forward to getting into it for a long time and now I am wondering why it is worse than the clerical job I was doing earlier", he is expressing his feeling of disappointment.The superior may respond by recognizing this feeling by stating "you feel disappointed because the new job has not been what you expected". This mirroring back of the feeling serves many purposes. Paraphrasing does not mean "parroting". It is not just a repetition of what the subordinate has said but rather communicating and understanding that the superior has got the essence of what his subordinate is saying: that is paraphrasing.

Responding to meaning is recognizing the reason behind the feeling and helping the person see the meaning as it comes to you. The content in the statements made by the person gives meaning to the feelings expressed. While responding to meaning you first state the feeling and give the content of the feeling with a word "because" before it. In the response given in the above para "you feel disappointed…..." is the response to feeling, and"because the new job hasn't been what you expected" is the response to meaning.

When we hear another, we tend to respond in five typical ways, viz,

a) Advisory or Evaluative, where we tend to pass judgmental statement indicating some standards which is acceptable or not acceptable, good or badand accordingly give advice.

b) Interpretative response, where we attempt to make an analysis of the individual and state as to what we think as the deeper level at which the person is operating. In other words, we tend to interpret the motive behind the statement.

c) In probing response we attempt to gain more information through the asking of the question or attempt to make the person say more about the problem.

d) In supporting response, we attempt to reassure and comfort the employee in his doubts or fears.

e) In an understanding response we tend to reflect back to the individual the contents and some of the feeling tone of his statement so as to check our understanding of the situation.

It is important to remember that any one of these ways of responding is not necessarily good or bad and each might be appropriate to different kinds of situations.

3.Guiding

Guiding is a technique the Manager uses to motivate or help the employee toplan or improving his performance on the job. This can take a number of formsfrom advice giving to building of decision making skills.

The purpose of guiding is to bring about constructive change with reference tothe employee's performance on the objectives to be achieved. For this reason guiding is the most important stage in the counselling process.

While keying and responding help the employee in self-exploration and therebyto understand himself, guiding focuses on the actual action steps that need to be taken for improvement.

This involves

    (i) identifying goals

    (ii) planning activities for achieving these goals.

A frequent reason why counselling does not succeed is that it stays at the keyingand responding stage. If the superior only listens, responds and is warm and respectful to the subordinate but does nothing in relation to work goals and plans he will be partially ineffective in the counselling process.

Effective guiding is therefore important and it requires that the superior should:

    (i) know enough about the subordinate and his problems,

    (ii) understand the relation between these problems and the subordinate's job performance, and

    (ii) develop plans for improvement jointly with the subordinate.

REFERENCES

1.***Brown, R.D.*** (1988); Performance appraisal as a tool for staff development; New Directions for Student Services No. 43; San Francisco: Jossey-Bass.

2.***Daughtrey, A.S., & Ricks, B.R.*** (1988); Contemporary supervision: Managing people and technology; New York: McGraw- Hill.

3.***Janosik, S.M., Creamer, D.G., Hirt, J.B., Winston, R.B., Saunders, S.A, & Cooper, D.L.*** (2003);Supervising new professionals in student affairs: A guide for practioners; New York, NY: Brunner-Routledge.

4.***Kessler, H. W.*** (2003); Motivate and reward: Performance appraisal and incentive systems for business success; Great Britian: Curran Publishing Services.

5.***Maddux, R.B.*** (1993); Effective performance appraisals: Third edition. Menlo Park, California: Crisp Publications Inc.

6.***McKirchy, K.*** (1998); Powerful performance appraisals: How to set expectations and work together to improve performance; National Press Publications: Franklin Lakes, NJ.

7. *University of CA- Berkeley* (2004, January);Conducting effective performance appraisals: Tips for supervisors. Administrator. Berkeley: California: Magna Publications, Inc.

8. *Werther, William B., Jr., and Keith Davis* (1989); Human Resources and Personnel Management. 3rd ed. New York: McGraw-Hill.

9. *Richard C. Grote* (1996), The Complete Guide to Performance Appraisal, AMACOM Div American Mgmt Assn.

10. *T.V. Rao* (2004), Performance Management and Appraisal Systems: HR Tools for Global Competitiveness, Sage Publications Pvt Ltd.

11. *Pulakos, Elaine* (2009); Performance Management: A NewApproach for Driving Business Results. Chichester, UK: Wiley.

12. *Akampurira Abraham* (2010);The effectiveness of teachers' performance appraisal in secondary schools in Kabale Municipality; Munich, GRIN Publishing GmbH.

13. *Dick Grote*(1996);The Complete Guide to Performance Appraisal; AMACOM, USA.

14. *Corey Sandler & Janice Keefe*(2003); Performance

Appraisal Phrase Book: The Best Words, Phrases, and Techniques for Performance Reviews; Adams Media.

15. *Mike Deblieux* (2003); Performance Appraisal Source Book- A Collection of Practical Samples; Society for Human Resource Management.

16. *T V Rao* (2004); Performance Management and Appraisal Systems: HR Tools for Global Competitiveness; Response Books-A Division of Sage Publication, New Delhi.

17. *PremChadha*(2003); Performance Management: It's About Performing - Not Just Appraising; Macmillan Publishers India Ltd.

18. *T. Venkateswara Rao & Raju Rao* (2020); 360 Degree Feedback and Performance Management System, Volume 1;Excel Books, New Delhi, India.

19. *Ravinder Shukla*(2009); Talent Management: Process of Developing and Integrating Skilled Workers; Global India Publications.

20. *Samuel A. Culbert& Lawrence Rout* (2010); Get Rid of the Performance Review!How Companies Can Stop Intimidating, Start Managing--and Focus on What Really Matters; Grand Central Publishing

21.http://www.vng-international.nl
22.http://www.hr.vcu.edu
23.http://www.uni.edu

www.ingramcontent.com/pod-product-compliance
Lightning Source LLC
Chambersburg PA
CBHW072310200526

45168CB00014B/1198